TED LEWIN
STABLE

Rb
Flash Point

A NEAL PORTER BOOK
ROARING BROOK PRESS
NEW YORK

A long time ago there was a stable in Brooklyn.
It was a time in America when horses did
just about everything.

They took people to the beach.

They pulled trolleys,

milk wagons,

and ice wagons.

They even pulled other horses.

They pulled steam fire engines.

But then things began to change,
and horses started to disappear from city streets.

By the 1960s the last ones were gone.

The old stable is still there in Brooklyn. It is one of
the last of its kind: a living, breathing, hay-burning
relic of a bygone era, crowded by huge high-rise
condos going up all around it. It is now called
Kensington Stables and is home to thirty-seven
horses. To step into the stable is to step
back in time.

There is a retired carriage horse named Margaret. There are Genie and Snickers, very popular with the kids, and an alpha mare named Stardust who holds the place together. There is Sign Me Up, and Katie, and Emma, called a "flea-bitten" mare because her coat is flecked with gray.

There's Spin Doctor, Florida, Fergus, and Spider, named for the spider web markings on her back caused by rain rot. There is a furry little pony named Chip, and Tonka, a big black horse with a white blaze who came from the Bronx. There is a horse with the mysterious name of Invisible. And horses with edible names like Marshmallow, Fudge, S'mores, fat little Butterscotch, Spice, who has bad legs, and Marzipan who is blind in one eye. And there's Oreo who was born in the stable. His mother's name was Cookie.

The stable is owned by a man named
Walker. He sits on a wooden box in his
"office" at the entranceway of the stable.
He constantly refers to the tattered notebook
on his lap that holds the list of reservations.
He is like a circus ring master as he organizes
pony rides, riding lessons, trail rides in the park,
and ponies being sent off in trailers to street
fairs and pony parties.

Horses are led out the door for trail rides.
"Coming out!" or "Going home!" they yell in the
narrow entranceway that's only big enough for
one horse at a time. Their hooves clip clop on the
pavement as they did a hundred years ago.

Out front ponies are washed and brushed so they "smell nice" for the kids eagerly awaiting their first time ever on the back of a pony.

The place whinnies and snorts with activity.
They like to say here, "When something
bothers you, go in a stall and hug a horse."

The farrier comes once a week,
a huge man named Hannaberry who's been
shoeing horses "longer than I can remember."

On sunny days lessons are given in the nearby
park. To get there you have to cross a busy traffic
circle. Eight-year-old Eva is taking her third lesson
on Marshmallow. At the traffic circle Ryka, her
instructor, runs out into the street waving
her arms. Cars slow to a halt. Clip clop come
Eva and Marshmallow past the big bronze statue
called "The Horse Tamers" into the green
quiet of the park.

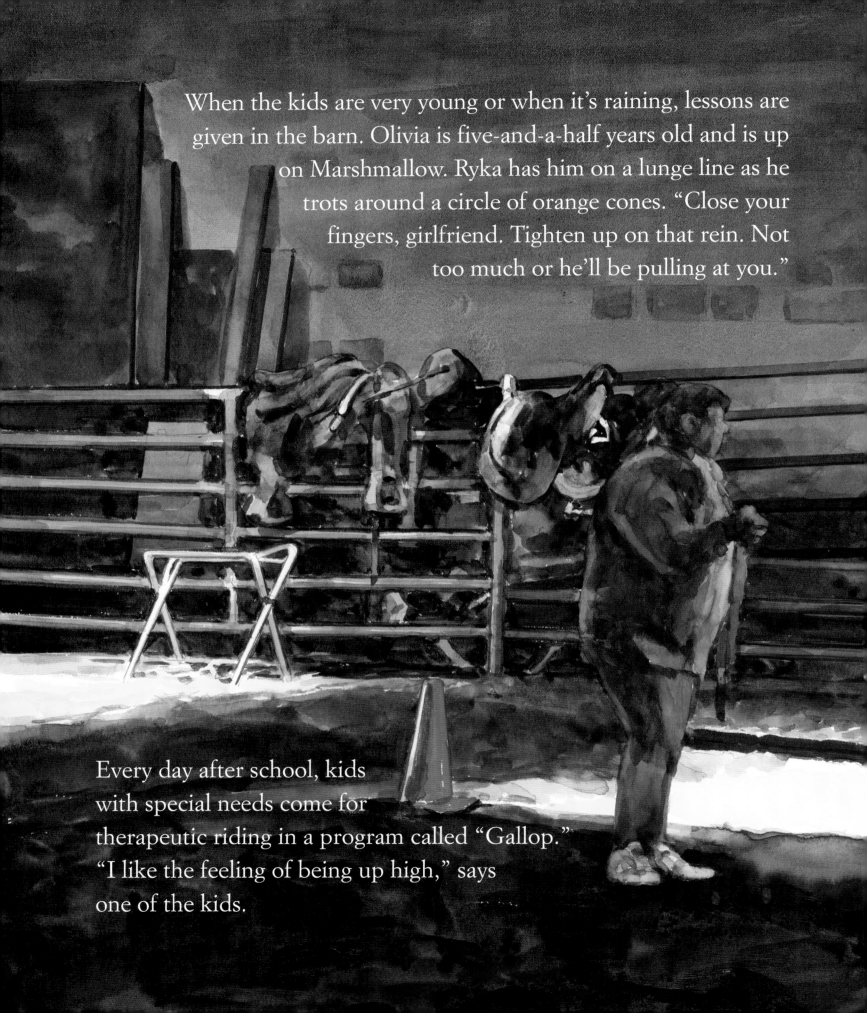

When the kids are very young or when it's raining, lessons are given in the barn. Olivia is five-and-a-half years old and is up on Marshmallow. Ryka has him on a lunge line as he trots around a circle of orange cones. "Close your fingers, girlfriend. Tighten up on that rein. Not too much or he'll be pulling at you."

Every day after school, kids with special needs come for therapeutic riding in a program called "Gallop." "I like the feeling of being up high," says one of the kids.

It's time to load the trailer. First up the ramp is Chip, who is stuffed in front under the hay bale. Then S'mores. Finally Fergus, who is last but certainly not least.

Then off they go to the annual autumn festival at a nearby day school where the children will ride them, pet them, and love them all day.

On a crisp fall day, it's time to hitch Fergus to the carriage for a wedding. "When we first got our carriage," says Walker, "Fergus looked at it as if to say 'At *last*, I've got something to pull.'"

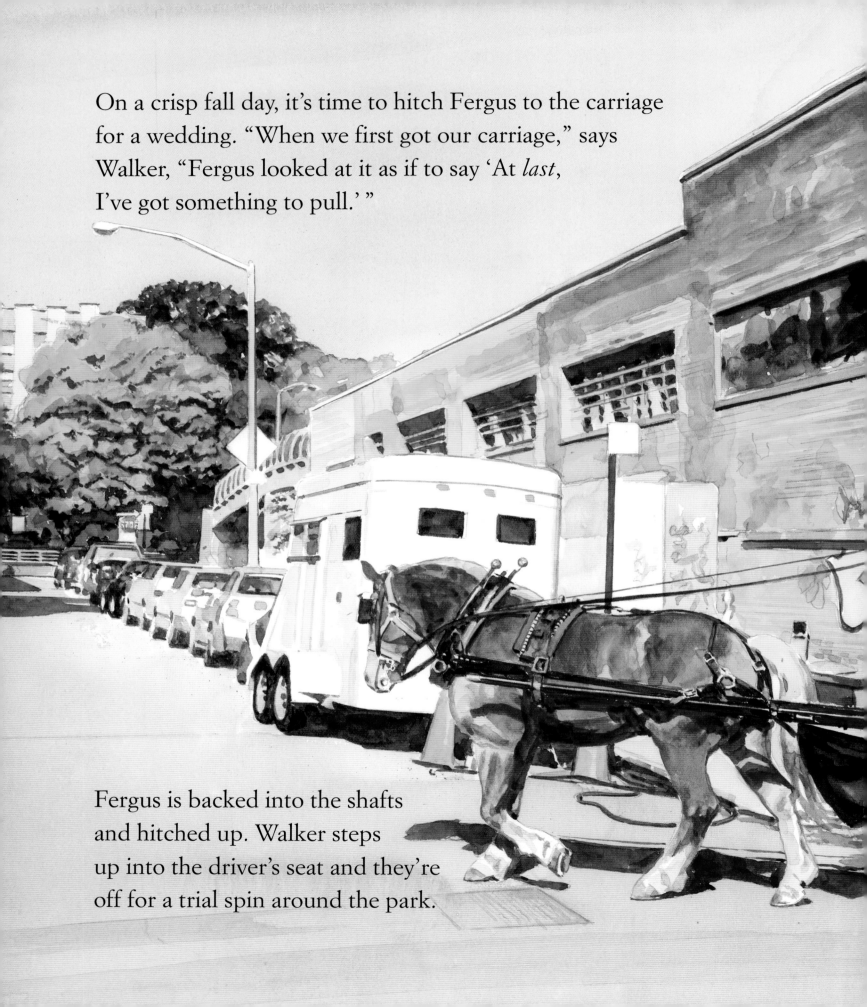

Fergus is backed into the shafts and hitched up. Walker steps up into the driver's seat and they're off for a trial spin around the park.

Watching the carriage pull away you can almost forget the huge buildings going up all around the little stable. What will become of these horses and the people who love them if the wrecker's ball finally comes?

CLIP CLOP

CLIP CLOP

CLIP CLOP

Carmen

Psi

Miracle

A NOTE FROM THE AUTHOR

In 1880, New York City and Brooklyn had a combined horse population of one-hundred-and-eighty thousand. Today that number has fallen to less than five hundred. Now, former stables and carriage houses have taken on new lives as people's homes. Hitching posts can still be found along the tree-lined streets, and over a restaurant door, a carved stone horse's head marks a former black-smith's shop. All are reminders of a time when horses ruled the streets.

Oreo

Rocky

Spider

Emma

Invisible

Harley

Sign Me Up

Fergus

Brandy

Genie

Snickers

Butterscotch

S'mores

Florida

Chip

Charm

Prince

Spin Doctor

Margaret

Katie

Kira

True

Fudge

Stardust

Lumpy

Marzipan

Phoebe

Merlin

Tiramisu

Spice

Bingo

Tonka

Marshmallow

Professor

To all horses past and present.
Special thanks to Walter Blankinship, Ryka,
and all the folks at Kensington Stable and Gallop.

Reference photo of the horse-drawn fire engine courtesy Brooklyn Historical Society.

Copyright © 2010 by Ted Lewin

A Neal Porter Book

Published by Flash Point, an imprint of Roaring Brook Press

Roaring Brook Press is a division of Holtzbrinck Publishing Holdings Limited Partnership

175 Fifth Avenue, New York, New York 10010

www.roaringbrookpress.com

Distributed in Canada by H. B. Fenn and Company Ltd.

Library of Congress Cataloging-in-Publication Data

Lewin, Ted.

Stable / Ted Lewin. — 1st ed.

p. cm.

"A Neal Porter book."

ISBN 978-1-59643-467-7

1. Kensington Stables (Firm)—Juvenile literature. 2. Horses—Housing—New York (State)—New York—
Juvenile literature. 3. Stables—New York (State)—New York—Juvenile literature. 4. Prospect Park
(New York, N.Y.)—Juvenile literature. I. Title.

SF285.35.L49 2010

636.1'0830974723—dc22

2009044431

Roaring Brook Press books are available for special promotions and premiums.

For details contact: Director of Special Markets, Holtzbrinck Publishers.

First Edition October 2010

Book design by Jennifer Browne

Printed in June 2010 in China by South China Printing Co. Ltd., Dongguan City, Guangdong Province

1 3 5 7 9 8 6 4 2